This book is dedicated to all who find Nature not an adversary to conquer and destroy, but a storehouse of infinite knowledge and experience linking man to all things past and present. They know conserving the natural environment is essential to our future well-being.

GREAT SMOKY MOUNTAINS
THE STORY BEHIND THE SCENERY®

Great Smoky Mountains National Park located in Tennessee and North Carolina, was established in 1926 to preserve a forested area rich in varied forms of life and one of the oldest uplands on earth.

by Rita Cantú

Rita Cantú, a graduate of the University of Arizona, has contributed significantly to the interpretive programs of our national parks. Her park service assignments have included many varied areas, with several years spent at Great Smoky Mountains National Park. Rita also performs and produces recordings of original music—her first record interpreted this Appalachian land and culture. Through her music and writings, she shares her appreciation of the scenic southern wonderland that is the Great Smokies.

Front and inside covers: Smoky Mountain vistas, Photos by David Muench. Title page: Trillium.
Photo by Zig Leszczynski/Animals Animals

Book Design by K. C. DenDooven

Fourth Printing, 1989
GREAT SMOKY MOUNTAINS: THE STORY BEHIND THE SCENERY. © 1979 KC PUBLICATIONS INC.
LC 78-78123. ISBN: 0-916122-59-X

*I*n the mist-sheltered hills of the Smokies lies a land of discovery: of nature—through her ancient forests, perennial streams, ephemeral flowers—and of self—through the way we receive the message that nature's elements impart. It is a place for everyone, a symphony that has no clanging crescendos, only the blending of many lifesongs into one harmonious world.

It's raining. You adjust your parka to stop the trickle from running down your neck and continue hiking. For two hours you've been walking in a swirling fog that makes ghosts of the trees beyond the trail. You pass a former cornfield, now grown up with pines, where a logpile and an old stone fence speak faintly of a time when the wilderness was held briefly at bay. You follow a stream flowing over moss-covered rocks and twining through ferns and wood-nettle, while the liquid song of a veery cascades down the scale like a stream tumbling down a mountain hollow.

Now you are in the heart of the Smokies. Hemlock and yellow poplars—virgin woodland, never logged—stand tall and patient in the rain. Just off the trail the mosses sink beneath your feet. The fragrances are rich and earthy: wet soil, fallen leaves, and the pungent hemlock needles. Silence—the timeless, somber celebration of a forest.

The trail becomes more difficult now. You clamber hand-over-hand through windfalls in the trail and through tangled rhododendron branches. No maze designed by man could be as maddening as this one. Finally you reach the ridge. Before you lies a grassy bald slowly growing in with berries, laurel, and flame azalea. Fifty years ago, settlers grazed their livestock each summer in these meadows. The trail winds along the mountaintop back into the forest, and gradually you notice other species—spruce and fir—along with the hemlock. The mist lies soft below the peaks, which spread before your gaze like rolling waves. The rain is gone. Time to sit and dream against a sun-warmed rock. The wind cools your shoulder blades where the pack rode. You've walked through rain, fog, and mist into sunshine, and you've traveled through communities of plants and animals that span half a continent—all in a day's hike in the Smokies.

The story of the Great Smoky Mountains is a story of time and forming rock, of growing forest and teeming life, of wilderness untouched by human hands, and of a land that even now is covering the scars of man's long use. It is the story of a forest rich with varied forms of life, of animals and plants balanced in survival in one of the most diverse and multi-specied forest areas of North America. It is a story of a temperate shelter from the glacial ice for the forests, of a mountain refuge for a band of Cherokee, and of a home for the mountain people. It is a story of hope and faith in the ability of humankind to recognize that "some things are best left as they are."

Preceding pages: The Smokies, enveloped in an amber mist. Photo by Ed Bower

ED BOWER

Th

Among the Cherokee Indians who live along th southeast boundary of the Smokies, there is legend that tells of the forming of these moun tains: In the beginning all animals and peopl lived in the sky. Below the sky was only th ocean. When their sky-vault became too crowded the People sent a little water beetle to look fo land in the ocean. When it could find no place t rest, it dived to the bottom and brought up a bi of mud, which grew and grew to form the earth

haping of the Land

While the earth was very soft a great buzzard was sent down to find a place dry enough for the People to live. As he flew over the Cherokee country he became very tired, and sinking low, his beating wings struck the soft earth, which hardened and formed the mountains and valleys that would be the Cherokees' first home.

Geologists have another answer to the question "How did the mountains get that way?", the deepest of the Smokies' mysteries. Myth and edu-

cated speculation are both part of the Smokies' story, for only when mystery and knowledge are combined can we come to fully understand and appreciate this special place.

The earliest beginnings of the Great Smoky Mountains were a time of drastic fluctuations of temperature and massive upheavals in the earth's crust. The bedrock of the Appalachian chain was probably a billion years old when it was metamorphosed and partially melted in the first mountain-

A geologic story unfolds among weathered rocks: Freezing and thawing fracture the mountains along ancient fault lines. A thin layer of soil collects in the cracks, in which new life establishes itself. The mountain breaking continues, as rhododendron plants and pine trees push their roots into the crevices, deepening and widening them.

DAVID MUENCH

building phase. When the ocean flooded in between eight- and six-hundred million years ago, much of the present bedrock was carried down from higher terrain and deposited in the ancient sea on top of sunken portions of the billion-year-old mountains. Much of the sedimentary material that came from the old terrain consisted of quartz, feldspar, and clay—from parent rocks of igneous as well as metamorphic material. The tremendous pressure of up to thirty thousand feet of sediment slowly combined with the chemical action of the water and cemented the murky floors of an ocean basin into rocks. This was the formation of the *Ocoee* series—the major rocks that form the underlying material of the Smokies.

During the Paleozoic era, between six-hundred and three-hundred million years ago, life began to venture out of the seas and onto the land. It was at this time that the seas deposited another, newer layer, along with shale and sandstone. This was limestone, the fossilized remains of marine animals and shells.

About four-hundred million years ago, all of this material was heaved from its basin by a series of major movements in the earth's crust, caused by gigantic internal pressures. This period, the time of mountain making, is called the *Appalachian Revolution.* The formation buckled, folded, cracked, and slid upon itself to form "thrust faults" of one rock mass upon another. Like a loosely crushed piece of paper, that which was

formerly flat was now peaked and wrinkled. It was a slow process, taking perhaps millions of years, and it all happened more than a hundred and twenty-five million years before the Rockies were formed!

Such revolutions in the earth's crust must have occurred several times. Mountains were formed, molded, eroded, and formed again. In the process of upheaval, the older layers of rock that had been deposited first slid over the younger rocks. Thus, in areas such as Cades Cove, a valley of Ordovician limestone (four-hundred million years old) is surrounded by Precambrian rock (six-hundred to eight-hundred million years old)—evidence of the intensity of the earth's upheaval. Cades Cove is called a "window," a naturally formed hole through which we can see rocks that are covered elsewhere. Here the younger limestone is exposed.

There are several caves, such as Gregory Cave in Cades Cove and Blowhole Cave in White Oak Sinks, that were formed by the slow seepage of ground water into the easily eroded limestone cavities. Some of the more rugged terrain, such as Charlies Bunion, the Chimney Tops, and the Sawteeth, was formed by the slaty, erosion-resistant rocks that were tilted on edge, creating a landscape of steep slopes and shallow soil cover that was especially vulnerable to landslides.

Through geologic as well as recent time, water played the major role in mountain sculpture. The patient agent of erosion gentles the jagged edges, rounds the peaks, and flows, falls, freezes, and thaws its way into every rocky crack and depression. We are spectators of the third section in this cyclic story of mountain making. First came the long ages of sediment deposition, followed by shorter periods of folding and upheaval in the earth's crust, followed by the present stage of water and wind erosion: mountain carving.

But the mountains are much more than great blocks of rock. They are covered by a thin veneer of soil that supports the plants that in turn support the animals. The mountains are a haven for many forms of life that would not be here were it not for the inexorable advance of the glacial ice sheets that never quite reached the Smokies but affected them with associated climatic changes.

In the temperate climate of the Arctotertiary period, deciduous forests were widespread across most of the earth. Then came the great ice sheets of the Pleistocene, driving all life in front of them in an exodus for survival. In this country the glaciers came as far south as what is now the Ohio River and then slowly began to recede. During this period, northern tree species such as spruce and fir became established, remaining in the high elevations when the glaciers retreated. The southern, warm-weather species moved downslope during the Ice Age and then returned to the higher peaks as more temperate growing conditions returned.

Boulders can still be found on the mountain slopes—evidences of the tremendous pressures of freezing and thawing during the glacial period. The processes of freezing and thawing have loosened blocks of bedrock and concentrated them in boulder fields, such as those on the Noah "Bud" Ogle nature trail, along the Cherokee Orchard drive, or along the Cove Hardwoods trail above the Chimney Tops picnic area. The boulders are still continuing their imperceptible march down the mountainside, as they have with each succession of freezing and thawing since the first intense glaciation periods pushed them away from their faulted bedrock on a higher ridge.

The formation of these mountains is not only a story of the geologic past, but a story of the present whims and climatic moods of nature. Much of the spectacular mountain scenery and, in some cases, the very survival of some species and animals is due to recent natural occurrences—catastrophes in man's short-term definition of things but a vital process in the long-term context of natural events. The Smokies landscape has been

DAVID MUENCH

Sunset at Clingmans Dome highlights the smooth, eroded surface of ancient rock laid down by seas almost a million years ago. Wind and water continue to sculpt the face of the mountain. In the climate of the Ice Age, the Smokies stood untouched by the grinding glaciers, providing a refuge for a rich diversity of plants and animals.

The craggy peaks of the Chimney Tops form a prominent landmark overlooking the Newfound Gap road from Gatlinburg to Cherokee. They are part of the Anakeesta *formation, as are most of the steep ridges and rugged pinnacles in the higher parts of the Smokies. The Anakeesta is characterized by weathered rocks made dark and rusty by the carbon and iron of this formation.*

Waves of mountains in a sea of time bathe the evening landscape in hues of haunting beauty.

formed and re-formed by natural phenomena throughout the recent ages—floods, windstorms, landslides, and forest fires.

On Mount LeConte, for instance, at least forty landslides occurred during a single thunderstorm in 1951 that dropped four inches of rain in an hour and flooded Gatlinburg as well. The enormous *V* slashed into the side of a mountain, easily visible from Newfound Gap Road, was also caused by that 1951 storm, together with the landslides of several succeeding years. The soil is but a thin carpet covering the rocky base of the mountains— a fragile layer that is easily swept away.

Yet some of the most scenic views are along the scars of recent landslides, from the Alum Cave Bluffs trail. A number of native plants depend upon open areas of full sunlight for their growth; the meadowlike conditions of a recent slide provide the habitat for such rare species as grass-of-Parnassus and linear-leafed gentian. Other plants and wildflowers thrive upon old burn scars and slides, adding their colorful threads to the tapestry of the Smokies scene and brightening disturbed areas during spring and summer blooming periods.

Fire has played—and still plays—a vital role in the continuation of many species. The lightning-caused fire is essential to the survival of a healthy ecosystem. Some tree species, such as pines, regenerate better after forest fires. On the drier ridges, many shrubs and herbs flower profusely after a light burn. Wildlife also benefits from a burn.

Woodpeckers remove beetles from fire-killed trees, and bears feast on the improved blueberry crop. Deer browse on young succulent shoots that spring up from the charred bases of shrubs.

Windstorms play a vital role in forest regeneration. Some of the largest trees, such as yellow (tulip) poplars, require open sunlight to become established and thus may owe their size and growth to the openings provided by major blow-downs centuries ago.

What seems to be an unchanging scene is simply a system operating upon a different concept of time: the trees, standing as they have stood for centuries; the streams, constantly cutting their channels as they flow; the rain, gently falling; and the wind, softly sighing. All speak to us of a forest unchanging and primeval. We want to preserve it, and so we control fires, channel streams, dam rivers, build retaining walls, and curse the storm we can't control. Yet in the larger scheme, the flash flood is necessary to the course of streams, the fire to the regeneration of the forest, and the windstorm to the continuing succession of life. The wilderness is ultimately a dynamic system whose very existence *depends* upon change. It cares not at all whether we who measure time in the blinking of an eye call them catastrophes or not.

Man arrived upon a world seemingly complete. But the earth he lives on is still forming, still changing, still adapting. And the hand of man lies heavy on the land. Unwilling to bend to meet nature's short-term discomforts, unseeing (or uncaring) of his long-term effect upon the system, he molds and masters nature—but only temporarily. Such places as the Great Smokies remind us that we are part of a much larger whole and that change is constant, uncontrollable, and necessary. "Through a glass darkly" we see ourselves and our time frame against the mountains and their time, and we are humbled.

SUGGESTED READING

DOOLITTLE, JEROME. *The Southern Appalachians.* New York: Time-Life Books, 1975.
KING, PHILIP B.; NEUMAN, ROBERT B.; HADLEY, JARVIS B. *Geology of the Great Smoky Mountains National Park, Tennessee and North Carolina.* Geological Survey Professional Paper 587. Washington, D.C.: U.S. Gov't. Printing Office, 1968.

DAVID MUENCH

The Forested Slopes

The Smokies' greatest treasure is its forests. Harboring a variety of plant life unequaled in most temperate areas of the world, these complex communities of animals and plants are interdependent societies in which every plant, animal, and patch of soil is in some way tied to the rest. Over fourteen hundred species of flowering plants, including over a hundred species of trees, exist here, each one giving to and taking from the nurturing soil that sustains it, in a continuum of life and death.

Flame azalea. In June whole hillsides come alive with its brilliance.

ED COOPER

Because of its northeast-southwest orientation, the Smokies supports a number of habitats that would not be as varied if there were only a cold north face and a warm south face to the exposure of the mountainsides. The height and ruggedness of the mountains are other reasons for the diversity of plant communities found here. Elevations range from 840 feet at the mouth of Abrams Creek to 6,642 feet at Clingmans Dome. The mountains are shaped by constant rain, with ridges that branch and subdivide to create drainage systems of over seven hundred miles of streams. The average annual rainfall in the Smo-

kies ranges from about eighty inches on the peaks to about fifty inches in the valleys.

The forest variety has been increased by recent human history also. By the time the Smokies was established as a national park, about sixty-five percent of the area it covered had been logged, and over six thousand families had cleared their patches of land, built their homes, and grown their crops on the land. Although at first glance this mountain wilderness seems pristine, most of the lower-elevation forests are fields and logged-over areas recovering from the impact of human use. But thirty-five percent of the park's 520,000 acres represents the most extensive virgin forest remaining in the East—a message of optimism at society's recognition and protection of wild lands, or a sad commentary upon its "twelfth-hour" tendency to save them, depending upon one's viewpoint. There is no disputing the importance of this frighteningly small portion of wilderness, however.

Botanists classify the Smokies' flora into many different vegetation communities. Each community is characterized by typical species of trees and shrubs and flowering herbs. What determines what grows where? Primary factors are elevation, moisture (or lack of it), and exposure. Different kinds of trees grow in different areas, depending upon the kind of environmental factors they need. The kinds of trees that grow in the forest determine the "understory type" of plants that grow among them. Two of the vegetation communities described in the park are unique to this region: the *heath balds* and the *cove-hardwood forests*.

The hushed beauty of the cove-hardwood forest creates a natural cathedral in which to pause and meditate. The leaf mosaic of hemlock, yellow poplar, maple, and birch filter the sunlight to a muted glow, but an occasional sunbeam eludes the screen of leaves to illumine and warm the forest floor.

These meadowlike spaces in the forests are grass "balds," often adorned by summer blooms of rhododendron (pictured) and flame azalea.

Heath balds (called locally "laurel slicks" or "hells," depending upon whether one is viewing them or hiking on them) are comprised almost entirely of rhododendron, laurel, sand myrtle, and azalea. Viewed from afar, they appear meadowlike and lush in the high elevations—"bald" patches of soft, green carpets topping forested slopes. Viewed from a vantage point on hands and knees (the only possible way to get through them), they are a wild tangle of rough and twisted stems. In early summer they bloom with an unrestrained magnificence. Rhododendron colors range from pinkish white to intense purple, interspersed with flame azaleas in vivid fireshades and the soft whites of mountain laurel. Every June the roads and trails are filled with visitors on pilgrimages to "see the rhododendron in bloom."

The cove-hardwood forest is similar to the magnificent forests that once blanketed the eastern United States, Europe, and Asia before the Ice Age. In this forest, which exists at low to mid elevations (to 4,500 feet), is found the greatest diversity of tree species, shrubs, and wildflower displays of the Smokies. The cool, sheltered coves of the mountain valleys provide all the necessary factors for growth of many species: rich soil, abundant rainfall, and a mild climate.

More than eighty kinds of trees abound in the cove-hardwood forest, most of them broadleaved rather than needle-leaved species. Buckeye, basswood, maple, yellow poplar, oak, and silverbell are at home here and reach tremendous size in areas of virgin growth. The Ramsey Cascade and Porters Creek trails in the Greenbrier section of the park, as well as Rainbow Falls and Grotto Falls trails along the Cherokee Orchard road, wind through the excellent stands of cove-hardwood species. Some fine stands can be found on the North Carolina side above Smokemont and in the Raven Fork area.

Below the tree canopy in the filtered sunlight grow many shade-tolerant shrubs and smaller trees such as dogwood, rhododendron, azalea, hydrangea, and a variety of woody vines. In spring the forest floor is covered with delicate wildflowers: trillium, toothwort, spring beauty, fringed phacelia, dutchman's-breeches, trout lily, squirrel corn. The names sound like characters from a magic kingdom, and some flowers look like them, too. The forest floor is carpeted with mosses

Catawba rhododendron, brilliant blooms of midsummer

Mountain laurel, blossoms of delicate purity

Dutchman's-breeches, whimsical garments on an elfin clothesline

Pink lady's-slipper, endangered elsewhere, thriving in the park

Perhaps the strongest identifying characteristic of the Smokies is its world-renowned diversity of wildflowers. The rich soil, gentle climate, and abundant rainfall provide an excellent habitat for over 1,400 species of flowering plants. Of the species that bloom here, many occur only in the Smokies, and some others are not usually found this far south.

A butterfly, the painted lady, gathering nectar

The tiny, dark-eyed junco is at home in summer's luxuriant foliage or winter's crystalline simplicity.

The familiar gray squirrel is a symphony of form and subtle color in his tree habitat.

and fungi, flowering plants, and tree seedlings. This is nature's cradle; here she reclaims her own and nurtures a new generation.

The cycle of life and death is evident on every hand; a fallen tree is soft and spongy, becoming one again with the soil. Overhead persistent drumming tells of a sapsucker busily hammering on a woodland high-rise—a standing snag. His busy perforations, like a barber-pole stripe, spiral the trunk. Just inside the flaking outer bark are winding trails where beetles feed. A squirrel or owl might poke its head around a higher limb, and a hollow snag might serve as a winter den for a weary bear. There is a timeless stillness here, an awesome presence of unseen life that heeds a clock different from ours. Yellow poplars stand as they have for centuries, so wide five men could not join hands around them. They have seen the coming and passing of the Cherokee, mountain settler, and modern urbanite, each seeking something different from the forest where they stand, and each leaving richer than they came.

Higher up the mountain slope is the northern hardwood forest, dominated by broad-leaved trees such as beech and birch, more typical of the northern United States. These forests also provide a habitat for some of the finest wildflower displays in the park. In midsummer the northern hard-woods that grow along the Newfound Gap road and Clingmans Dome road can be easily distinguished by the lighter green, almost lacy pattern of beech leaves and heavier leaf patterns of the other hardwoods interspersed with darker spruce and fir.

The spruce-fir forest is another distinctive feature of the Smokies. It grows and flourishes a thousand miles south of where it would be were it not for the march of glaciers long ago. The erect needles and angular form of the red spruce and Fraser fir speak of a harsher life than most forest species have. Growing at elevations over 4,500 feet, the spruce and fir are often hidden in cold, swirling mist. Those on exposed slopes often appear "flagged," sculpted by ice, snow, and harsh winds that deform their branches on the windward side. Although the two trees appear to be similar from a distance, at close range they are easily distinguishable. The needles of the Fraser fir are green on top and silvery-gray underneath, and the cones grow in an upright position, making the branches look like candelabra. Spruce needles are shiny-green on both sides; the cones hang downward.

Understory vegetation is much more limited here, caused in part by the shade and in part by the acidic tannin of the conifers imparted to the

TOM BRAKEFIELD/ANIMALS ANIMALS

ZIG LESZCZYNSKI/ANIMALS ANIMALS

"Flagging" aptly describes the condition of these Fraser-fir branches, which have been deformed by wind on their exposed sides.

soil from fallen needles. However, several shrubs—such as the mountain cranberry and the black-berry—and wildflowers—such as trillium, wood sorrel, and bluet—also make their homes in this mysteriously beautiful forest. Other trees found here include yellow birch, pin cherry, mountain maple, and serviceberry.

The animal life of the spruce-fir forest is also more typical of northern climes. The red squirrel, known among mountain dwellers as the "mountain boomer" because of its incessant chattering, shares its habitat with the red fox, deer mouse, flying squirrel, and a variety of birds, such as the junco, veery, and winter wren. One might glimpse a raven soaring above the trees; similar in appearance to the crow but larger, the raven is a shy and solitary bird—a symbol of the harsh, unspoiled mountain peaks.

On the mountains' drier slopes in mid and low elevations, the pines and oaks predominate, preferring the dry, exposed ridges to the lush coves. These forests are more typical of plant

A downy woodpecker fills the anxious beaks of her hungry young.

W. GRIFFIN/ANIMALS ANIMALS

Sturdy forest monarchs stand tall above the tangled undergrowth of a dynamic, ever-changing community: the successional forest. Heavy transpiration from the thick forest is thought to be one cause of the mountains' characteristic smokiness.

ED BOWER

communities found elsewhere in the southern region. They contain such plants as hickory, red maple, dogwood, laurel, and rhododendron.

Although the botanists and other classifiers might find it frustrating, the natural world does not break down well into carefully constructed terms and categories; it is difficult to specifically separate one forest type from another or to pinpoint the elevation, slope, and conditions at which the forest type suddenly changes. Although a "climax" or constant-species forest stage is fairly stable, most forests are in some stage of succession, progressing from one predominant species to another.

For example, in a certain area where the settlers left the land they had cleared for raising crops and building homes, a complex successional pattern began as the fields returned slowly to forest. Over a period of fifty to a hundred years, various plant species grew, died, and were replaced by others. Grasses that filled the empty fields were replaced by short-lived herbaceous and woody plants, replaced in turn by woody shrubs and trees that flourished in the open sunlight, and replaced finally by shade-tolerant species that grew under the shadows of the adult, sun-loving trees above them. Thus it was that the land reverted to the climax forest that originally greeted the first settlers, and the cycle is complete—until a fire, windstorm, landslide, or human being disrupts the system again.

WILDLIFE OF THE SMOKIES

It is the diversity of habitat that is probably the single most important aspect of Great Smoky Mountains National Park. The variety which is provided by the many plant communities makes for a great diversity of animals as well. Within the park there are about fifty species of mammals and over two hundred species of birds, nearly eighty of which make the Smokies their home in winter as well as in summer. In addition, there are about forty species each of reptiles and amphibians, and about seventy species of fish.

The feature of the park that undoubtedly holds the greatest interest to Smokies' visitors is the mammals, and of them all the black bear wins the popularity prize. The only species of bear in the eastern United States, the black bear is an engaging animal. Bears are wild animals and should not be approached closely and never fed. Contacts with humans and their food turns wild bears into pathetic beggars—unhealthy for the bear and potentially dangerous to humans.

16

The black bear, symbol of the Smokies, has thrived under the protection of the national park, although elsewhere it is a much hunted and beleaguered animal. The cubs are born blind and hairless, each about the size of a young rabbit, and leave the den about two months later. The fiercely protective mother—an indulgent parent but a stern disciplinarian—is never very far from her audacious, inquisitive cubs. Graceful and engaging or powerful and formidable—it all depends upon the circumstances of your meeting!

Yet, of a total population estimated at between four and six hundred black bears in the park, the proportion of those who have lost their cautiousness in regard to humans is surprisingly small. Fewer than five percent of this population are seldom if ever glimpsed by picnickers or backpackers. The typical bear disappears from sight at the first scent of a human. Ironically, it is this same small percentage that provides most of the visitor satisfaction of having "seen a bear." Any old bear.

Meanwhile the other ninety-five percent go on about their business in the inaccessible and isolated reaches of the park. In summer they feast on blackberries, raspberries, huckleberries, and blueberries. The cubs frolic and grow (an adult female will have twin cubs every two years), building strength and coordination in games of tag, tumbling, and wrestling. In autumn they forage for acorns and hickory nuts, building up reserves of fat to see them through the winter. As winter nears, they return to their home ranges and their dens—most likely in hollow trees twenty to sixty feet above ground—for the cold months.

Bears do not actually hibernate; they may wake and roam around on warm, sunny days. But

STEPHEN J. KRASEMANN

during the winter their gastrointestinal tracts shut down. They don't urinate, defecate, eat, or drink during their denning period. As spring warms the woods, the bears again begin to roam, living off their body fat, still stored from last fall, while they hunt for a meager repast of the leaves and stems of herbaceous plants. Not until the summer berry crop will they again gain weight and live "the good life." Popular conceptions of the bears are probably justified in one thing: There is no better symbol for the wilderness areas of the East than the engaging and intelligent black bear.

One of the best places for viewing wildlife is in a partially open, partially wooded area. In the lower fields and meadowlands one can occasionally encounter this "edge-zone effect." Areas of open land surrounded by wooded areas will always have a greater abundance of wildlife than will forest or meadowland alone, as there is a greater variety of food and cover, important elements in a life of continual struggle for survival.

Cades Cove, for example, is one of the best areas in the park for viewing wildlife. In the early mornings or late evenings one may see deer grazing peacefully among the pastures and cabins. Wild turkey gather along the edges of the forest, and groundhogs or "whistle pigs" often perch above their burrows or by the roadside, disappearing with a shrill whistle if the occasion seems to warrant it.

Deeper in the forest, other wildlife abounds, although not so easily seen as the dwellers at the

forest's edge. The chipmunk and the gray squirrel make their presence known, the former by scampering quickly across the trail, the latter by its angry "chrrr!" of territoriality. At dusk one might see a fox peek out through the underbrush or run across the road, and a very quiet, very lucky hiker might be rewarded with the glimpse of a bobcat. Many of the woodland denizens are nocturnal and less likely to be seen. However, many a backpacker has been visited by camp marauders such as raccoons, and 'possums, and can attest to the sharp scent of skunks!

Although the park has a varied reptile population, it has only two poisonous snakes—the copperhead and the timber rattlesnake. The rattler has yellowish to blackish colorings. The copperhead's skin pattern is an hourglass design along a brownish body; it is sometimes found near water and in old log piles. Very few hikers will ever encounter either of these vipers, but when one does turn up, the best course of action seems to be to give it a wide berth. It will go its own way if the hiker goes his. *All* animals, even those that some consider less than likeable, are protected within the national park.

The Smokies is a bird watcher's paradise, although the density of the trees camouflages the birds so effectively that they are often difficult to identify by sight. In the higher elevations a variety of northern species abound. Flycatchers and juncos, wrens and ravens make their homes in the inaccessible reaches of the Smokies. In early autumn the song of winter wrens brings the still forest to life. On summer evenings the lengthening shadows are heralded by the full-throated

Wild turkeys are often seen in Cades Cove.

The red fox, infrequently residing in the Smokies, can be distinguished from the gray fox by its black legs and feet and by its white-tipped tail.

19

Mourning dove, with young

Immature red-tailed hawk, assuming a defensive posture

Cedar waxwings, a family occasionally seen in the Smokies

choruses of wood thrushes, veeries, and Carolina wrens. At almost any season the resonant, low, thumping sound of the ruffed grouse may be heard throughout the forest. The sound accelerates into a fast drumming as the chicken-sized bird, camouflaged in fallen leaves, balances against a log and beats the air with its wings. In every season the forest is a microcosm of life, a complex society of large and small, predator and prey, all with a role to play and a strand to build to support the web of life.

The story of the habitat and dwellers of the Smoky Mountains would be incomplete if it did not deal especially with its streams. The Great Smokies receives more annual precipitation than almost any other area in the contiguous United States. More than half this rainfall seeps into the ground or is captured as runoff in the streams. The rest evaporates or is used directly by plants. Streams are the voices and the laughter of the mountains. They bubble as springs from the surface and flow down the slopes in trickles or in torrents. Such springs have brought many a wandering mountaineer back to his old home for the taste of the sweet water, a return perhaps explained only by a cryptic comment about the city when he came: "Water's bad." The streams and rivers, like the forests where they flow, support some of the richest flora and fauna of any region of similar size and elevation in North America.

Smallmouth bass, sculpins, trout, and numerous small species of fish abound. On a clear day one can glimpse many different species in a limpid pool, swimming slowly or pointing, motionless, upstream against the current. They hang suspended, deceptively still, until a hapless insect comes within range. Then in a silvery streak fish and insect are gone.

There are three species of trout in the park, but only one of them is native, the southern Appalachian brook trout, called affectionately "spec" or "brookie" by local folks. A glistening, greenish silver with brilliant, reddish-orange spots and a streak of orange branded across its lower side, the brook trout is indeed a beautiful sight.

The spec has lived in these streams for several centuries. But eventually man introduced a force into the streams with which the brook trout could not cope—logging; the hills, then denuded, flowed into the stream, muddying the water and causing a decline of the trout. Then another, more powerful force for the brookie's demise was introduced—the rainbow trout, stocked in streams by loggers to improve the fishing.

Nowhere in the Smokies is the cycle of life more in evidence than in one of its clear-flowing mountain streams. Fed first by rains, then by rivulets down the higher slopes, the torrent gathers momentum and rushes through the forest, nurturing it in spite of its haste. Moisture is pulled through roots and soil by thirsty plants that continue the cycle through transpiration. Clouds return the moisture to the earth and streams as life-giving rain.

The problem of siltation was stopped when the National Park Service put an end to logging. But the rainbow trout remained, and it is slowly pushing higher upstream into the brook trout's domain. It seems the spec can't compete with the larger, more aggressive rainbow or the more recently introduced brown trout. In the areas where the species overlap, the brook trout seems doomed. Its population has been so seriously reduced that it is now considered an endangered species in the Smokies. Its future is indeed uncertain.

The streams are home to a variety of aquatic life, in addition to fish. Above the surface dart dragonflies, mayflies, and stoneflies. On the surface skate water striders and beetles. Submerged and feeding on the rich algal life of the stream, caddisfly larvae are encased in wrappings of twigs or pebbles, so that they look like miniature mummies. The water-scavenger beetle swims underwater, like a diver, and takes along its own air supply trapped in the bubble that it carries with it.

Alongside small streams and under rocks that hide all but an upraised, glowing pair of

eyes, dwells another form of life. Unless you are simply sitting and staring at nothing in particular, you might miss this streamside dweller. Slowly it dawns upon you that *something* is staring back! A really curious type might sink to hands and knees in the middle of the stream and peer into the rocks along the muddy edge to discover *lots* . . . of pairs . . . of eyes . . . staring back! The eyes may belong to members of the nearly two dozen species of salamanders that live in the park. (Or they may belong to something else!)

It is widely known that the Smokies is the "salamander capital" of the United States. It has more species of salamanders than any other area in the country. Salamanders are quizzical and friendly looking amphibians, ranging from the

Curious eyes peering from hidden streamside niches could belong to a salamander

—or a snake!

Northern water snake

The small, steep headwater streams of the Smokies provide excellent habitats for many streamside dwellers, such as salamanders. But these rain- and spring-fed streams are extremely turbulent and do not support as many algae, fish, and other forms of aquatic life as do lower-elevation streams.

smallest known species, the pygmy (about two inches long) to the largest, the hellbender (which may reach a length of twenty-nine inches). Smokies streams are a little-noticed arena of life, perhaps less familiar than those aboveground but every bit as fascinating and lovely just the same.

The Threat of Exotics

The temperate climate and diverse habitat of the Great Smokies make it an ideal home for many living things. Among those who know it as home are a number of *exotics*, non-native species that have been introduced through human activity. These animals and plants seriously alter natural ecosystems by destroying habitats or crowding out the less adaptable native species that would otherwise still occupy that particular ecological "niche."

Often unaware of the damage exotics cause to a delicately balanced natural ecosystem, man has introduced them into new territory. Once the damage is discovered, it is often too late to return to the "natural order"—at least without a struggle. Thus we are faced with the frustrating results of our own ignorance.

The largest of these unwanted species is the European wild hog, which was introduced to the area in 1912 and entered the park in the 1940s. Hogs in the park uproot and destroy acres of fragile wildflower communities in their search for grubs and roots just below the soil surface. Biologists attribute a variety of problems to them, includ-

Black-chinned red salamander, one of about two dozen species in the park

The slimy salamander, camouflaged in sun and shadow

The green frog; a compelling gaze

The five-lined skink, a graceful study in form

Overleaf: A mountaineer's rustic cabin and fence in Cades Cove define a simple way of life in a setting of grandeur.
Photo by Ed Cooper

Springtime splashes white blossoms on a smoky backdrop.

ing damaged ecosystems, polluted streams, reduced plant diversity, predation on small native animals, and competition with native species such as the black bear for natural foods such as acorns.

The red-and-brown patches of dying trees in the spruce-fir forests are caused by the balsam woolly adelgid, a tiny insect, almost microscopic. Introduced into this country by accident about 1900, it now occurs throughout North America and is slowly infecting and killing the mature Fraser fir trees in the Smokies. Researchers have not found a suitable method for its control. In time, the balsam woolly adelgid may destroy the entire adult Fraser fir population in the park.

Of the many species of exotic plants in the park, only a few are expanding fast enough to threaten native ecosystems. These plants usually grow in "disturbed" areas—perhaps in fields cleared by early mountain farmers or areas intruded upon by the building of roads and trails. The kudzu vine, a fast-growing plant brought from Asia for use in stabilizing stream banks and reducing soil erosion, was, like many such agricultural imports, too successful. Kudzu covers whole areas of trees. As the vine shades trees from the light, it eventually causes their death. Only through continuous control has the park been kept relatively free of this ghost-shroud vine. The Japanese honeysuckle, planted by many mountain farmers along fence rows and near cabins, now is widespread in the park and flourishes under a full-canopied forest, where it often forms a tangled mat that shades out native wildflowers.

In 1904 an inconspicuous fungus was imported to New York from China—piggybacked on a Chinese chestnut tree. About twenty years later this fungus, the "chestnut blight," came to the Smokies. By 1938 the American chestnut tree, symbol of native American forests, was almost completely gone from the park—victim of this exotic fungus.

In some cases, the disruption of natural order has been caused more directly by man. In the Great Smokies a number of wild animals used to roam freely until the Indians and the mountain settlers intentionally or accidentally reduced their numbers to nothing. Such is the case with the bison, killed off by the late 1700s, the American elk *(wapiti)*, gone by the 1840s, and the gray wolf and eastern mountain lion exterminated sometime around 1900. All of them once ranged the park area.

There are no immediate plans to reintroduce these larger animals back into the park; but several smaller species have already been successfully brought back and others are being studied for reintroduction. In recent years, the peregrine falcon and river otter have been released and are gaining a foothold. The fisher is among those under consideration.

The survival—or return—of native species such as the peregrine falcon, the bear, the otter, and a myriad of more common but equally important animals and plants infinitely enriches this park in the land of smoky mystery.

SUGGESTED READING

BROOKS, MAURICE. *The Appalachians.* Grantsville, West Va.: Seneca Books, 1965.

BROOME, HARVEY. *Out Under the Sky of the Great Smokies.* Knoxville: The Greenbrier Press, 1975.

FROME, MICHAEL. *Strangers in High Places.* New York: Doubleday and Co., 1966.

Autumn (at Laurel Creek) adds its brilliant tones to the endless variety of themes nature plays in this enchanting land.

Man in the Smokies

The procession of human wanderers through these hills presumably began with the crossing of the Bering Strait by primitive Asian hunters between fifteen and twenty thousand years ago. Small bands of these nomadic people came through the valleys and highlands of the mountains, leaving only spear points and scraping tools as signs of their passing. Some of these hunters may have stayed, evolving into the Cherokee, one of the largest tribes in North America. Most ethnologists believe the Cherokee derived from the Iroquois in the north, then split from that stock and began moving southward nearly a thousand years ago. They settled in the area of the Southern Appalachian chain (in what is now an eight-state region, bounded on the north by the Ohio River)

ED COOPER

WILLIAM A. BAKE

A few rails of fencing, some hand-hewn log buildings for family and livestock, and the unending forest and mountains beyond constituted the everyday world for generations of mountain people who made the Smokies their home.

and extended their territory to include half of what is now South Carolina and nearly all of Tennessee and Kentucky.

The birthplace of the Cherokee was the valleys of the Tellico and the Little Tennessee rivers, in the shadow of the Smokies. Kituwha, the first town, was located in the area of the present-day Deep Creek campground. In the heart of the Cher-

okee nation lay the great imposing range of the *Shaconage*, one of the many Cherokee words for the mountains, "the place of the blue smoke." For the most part, the Cherokee settled along the fertile valleys and river-bottoms at the foothills and in the shadows of the Smokies. They hunted the abundant game that dwelled along the mountain slopes.

The mountains provided not only material welfare, they also harbored the spirit of the tribe. There dwelled the "Little People," legendary keepers of the history of the Cherokee. Each year, in autumn, the wise men of the tribe camped for seven days and nights in the shadow of the Chim-ney Tops. They shared the legends of the tribe and told stories of the feats accomplished and knowledge gained during the past year. On the seventh day, as night fell, the men grew silent, waiting. From the woods the sound of music and dancing grew and soon the Little People came— to share the legends, dances, and songs that were older than any living man could remember. As dawn broke, the little people slipped away, leaving new legends to add to the old ones and staying safely within their dwelling places among the rocks of Shaconage for another year.

The Cherokee were a proud and primarily peaceful people, busy in the cultivating of their

WILLIAM A. BAKE

improving the hunting for the Cherokee. And so they may have set fire repeatedly to some areas. They fished the life-laden streams; they cleared the forest to cultivate their crops; they gathered wild herbs and plants for medicinal as well as domestic use.

THE WHITE MAN AND CHANGE

But slowly the sight of white men wandering through their mountain homeland became more common. In 1540 the Spanish explorer Hernando de Soto became the first white man to venture into this general area. In the mid-1700s, tales of a rich and fertile land drifted back to the Scotch-Irish, who were already feeling crowded in the middle Atlantic states, to the Germans, who had settled in Pennsylvania, and to restless English settlers. These were the people who made their homes in the fertile lands at the base of the mountains. Cherokee and European by turns battled and befriended each other.

With the coming of the white man, the life of the Cherokee began to change—slowly at first, then with a speed of urgency as the Cherokee attempted to live in harmony with their white brothers. Finally their customs crumbled with an uncontrollable speed—a culture's demise which was the result of an inevitable conflict with a way of life and expansion that overwhelmed and engulfed it. There was simply no chance for the smaller culture to hold its own against the tide. Only their tribal organization and various internal customs, such as dress, remained.

With the end of the Revolutionary War and the beginning of independence for the new country, the appetite of its citizens for new land was too voracious to be curbed by the presence of a few Indians. Treaty after treaty was made and broken, and the land where the Cherokee dwelled became smaller and smaller. Yet the Cherokee and their related tribes conformed to the ways of the white man more than most Indians did at that time. By the early 1800s they had formed a republican-type government and adopted a constitution patterned after that of the United States. And it was the Cherokee who accomplished a feat unequaled in human history: the design of an entire alphabet by one man, Sequoyah. Within

fields, hunting in the mountains, and the performing of ritualistic dances and celebrations. Their culture was rich with myth and natural symbolism yet curiously consistent with the ways of life that the white man soon would force upon them. The Cherokee worshiped only one deity, had a democratic system of government, and lived—even before the introduction of European ways—in mud-and-log structures (rather than in tepees as the Plains Indians did). Women held positions in government of the tribe, and men helped with some of the household duties.

Although the Cherokee lived their own way of life upon the land, the effect they made upon their surroundings was slight. Had their numbers been larger, it is possible that they, like the European settlers, might have made as lasting an impression upon the land. As it was, they used the forests, streams, and wildlife in much the same ways as the white settlers who followed them, only less intensively. They often drove game to open areas where it could be more easily hunted, and they perhaps started fires in order to panic the game into moving. Their fires, like those naturally caused, resulted in clearings in the forests that attracted other species of wildlife, thus

Trademark of the Southern Appalachian settlers, a split-rail fence follows a wagon trace in a sunburnished setting. An old-folk belief maintains that fence rails should be split only during the dark of the moon, to prevent them from warping or cracking.

ED BOWER

two years after Sequoyah had presented his alphabet to the Cherokee Council, there was a newspaper, *The Cherokee Phoenix*, and nearly everyone who spoke Cherokee could read and write!

But all their adaptability and patience with the white man's ways helped them but little when gold was discovered in Cherokee country and pressures to gain Indian land rose to a fever pitch. In 1828 all their land was confiscated, their press destroyed, their laws and constitution declared null and void. With the passage of the Removal Act in 1830 all southeastern tribes were ordered to "relocate" to Oklahoma, and the tragic history of the "Trail of Tears" began. Nearly twenty thousand people were marched overland, and a quarter of them died along the way.

But not all the Cherokee left their mountain home. About a thousand fled in small groups, taking refuge in the isolated slopes of the Smoky Mountains between Clingmans Dome and Mount Guyot. The army could neither extract nor coerce them—it couldn't even *find* them. So, after killing a group of Indians as an "example" to the others, the hideout bands were left alone.

Three years later, the U.S. Government allowed the Cherokee to return in peace to their old homeland and reclaim its borders. Their land area was reduced and their numbers drastically decimated, but the Cherokee had regained what they had fought and suffered for—their mountain birthplace. There they remain today, on the Qualla Reservation. And perhaps the Little People also still remain, keeping the legends of a proud people in the rocky shelter of Shaconage.

The Mountain People

Now the taming of the wilderness became the task of the Europeans. Although the lowlands in the shelter of the Smokies had been won, the highlands remained to be conquered. They were not as coveted. Soil was thin, slopes were too rocky to plow, and the trees in the massive forests were too thick to cut. But as generation followed generation, the tradition of parceling the father's land to each new-married son quickly exhausted what usable land there was in the fertile coves and valleys.

By 1795, the Oconaluftee River, Cataloochee Valley, and Forney Creek areas of North Carolina had been claimed by settlers, as had the Tennessee side of the Smokies. The town of White Oak Flats, later known as Gatlinburg, boasted its first child in 1802. Likewise, Greenbrier Cove had felt the plow, and settlers were pushing their way up the West Prong of the Little Pigeon River into Sugarlands Valley, as far up as the Chimney Tops. Cades Cove, one of the most scenic and fertile areas in the Smokies, saw its first land claim, probably the one made in 1818 by John Oliver.

By the mid-1800s many families were in their third generation of settlement. The only land left was higher in the mountains. As the Cherokee had done before them, the settlers cleared their land, raised crops, hunted game, and grazed their few head of livestock where they could. But in the mountains, the process of settlement was a continuous battle with the wilderness. Fields had first to be cleared of trees, then cleared of rocks. Often the trees were so large and numerous that, rather than cutting them, pioneers "girdled" them, gashing a deep wound all the way around the tree to stop the flow of sap. Skeletons of girdled trees stood for years in cultivated fields, then were cut and burned.

Some families, such as those living in Cades Cove, were fortunate to find meadows along the mountain ridges—grassy balds, mysterious clearings surrounded by forest. Some settlers cleared pastures along the mountaintop and then cut back any incoming growth to keep them open. Parsons Bald, Andrews Bald, Gregory Bald, and Spence Field are all named after the farmers whose livestock grazed on the balds each summer, or for the herd tenders, who lived an isolated existence half the year surrounded by their herds in swirling mists, with a view of the valley below them.

ZIG LESZCZYNSKI/ANIMALS ANIMALS
ED BOWER

Millwheels tell the story of man and the land— and of the water that nourishes them both. Dozens of them were once scattered throughout the coves and valleys in the Smokies. Some large mills, with overshot water wheels (such as Cable Mill), were designed to serve the needs of a whole community, but most common were the small tub mills that ground the corn or rye for a group of two or three families.

Nearly every mountain woman had her flower garden, usually planted close to the house. This cabin along the Noah "Bud" Ogle trail is one of the larger mountain dwellings, with a spacious front porch and window.

ED COOPER

KC DENDOOVEN

The materials of mountain life were simple. Cabins were made of matched logs, hand-hewn and jointed at the corners. Puncheon floors were of single boards three or more feet wide. Door latches of wood and leather greeted the homecomer, who climbed steps of half-cut logs to enter the house. The result of a mountain man's labor was more than a home, barn, or springhouse; it was a work of art and utility which reflected the pride and craftsmanship of its creator.

KC DENDOOVEN

KC DENDOOVEN

KC DENDOOVEN

Generations-old methods of milling and syrup-making are still a part of life in these mountains. Sorghum molasses was made in the fall. The sorghum cane was first crushed in horse-powered mills, squeezed, filtered, and then cooked in large vats for three to four hours. Local farmers brought their corn to be ground and bagged by the miller as it was needed for their families.

E. R. DEGGINGER, FPSA/EARTH SCENES

Life for the isolated mountain people was a self-sufficient existence of hard work from dawn to dusk. The independent mountain dweller had little contact with a community and little time to seek it. Each homestead provided for its own needs. Cabin, corncrib, fences, and spring house were built by hand, from logs cut and hauled on the family's land.

A typical family might have a dairy cow for milk; some chickens; horses, mules, or oxen to pull the plow; numerous hunting hounds; and a pig or two for the winter meat supply. Hunting provided most of the meat during the spring, fall, and summer. Men did the hunting, the clearing, and the plowing. Women prepared the food, carded, spun, sewed clothing, tended the vegetable garden, and made sure that food and clothing would be adequate to see them through each winter. Children picked berries and beans, gathered eggs, and quickly matured to fill the roles they had inherited when they were born.

But there was another element to life, the traditions and the social occasions, which although rare were faithfully attended. As the Cherokee had their myths, dances, gatherings, and religion, so too the mountain people had theirs. Oftentimes a social gathering was also a time of work, but if something had to be done, many hands made it easier. There were cabin and barn raisings, corn shuckings, and quiltings to provide mutual assistance and companionship. There were church meetings, gospel singings, reunions, baptisms, marriages, and funerals, all of which drew the tight-knit group of neighbors closer still.

Church events provided an emotional outlet of religious fervor to a people who were usually bound by a silent stoicism. Many of the mountain dwellers had strong, fundamentalist beliefs, among which was the conviction that dancing and fiddle playing were tools of the devil. To sing in a church or family setting, however, was quite another thing.

RON McCANN

Quilting, braiding, weaving, spinning, making natural dyes—all were handicrafts typical of the Smokies region. Quilt designs, like mountain speech patterns, reflected a homespun sense of poetry. Products of artistic patience and pride, they bore names such as "Grandmother's Garden," "Double Wedding Ring," "The Tree of Life," and "Bonaparte's March." The mountain woman took as much pride in her handiwork as the mountain man took in his woodworking and leathercraft. These crafts are still very much alive in the Smokies.

E. R. DEGGINGER, FPSA/EARTH SCENES

The garden was a central part of the mountain farmstead and the responsibility of the woman and her children. It provided such staples as corn, beans, cabbage, onions, potatoes, squash, and tomatoes. A well-tended garden assured the family of ample provisions during the winter.

STEVE WOODCOCK

STEVE WOODCOCK

STEVE WOODCOCK

"Tune up the fiddle and rosin up the bow!" The fiddle was a common sight at a social held after a barn-raising or bean-stringing, and family "play parties" gave young and old alike the chance to enliven the summer evening with song after a hard day's work.

The natural emotions of the mountain people overflowed in simple, unadorned singing styles, in haunting modal melodies, in hopeful hymns, and lonely ballads. In the Southern Appalachians, more than any other place, the songs that were old when the first settlers arrived survived and flourished through each generation. They lasted because people sang them—while working, while playing, while worshiping.

Today many of the songs and singings are still alive. Old folks and young come back to their family places in the Smokies—Cades Cove, Greenbrier, and Cataloochee—to make music, dance, or reminisce about a time—not really long ago—when the miller, the blacksmith, and the store owner served a thriving community. In the summer or fall, the sound of "do-mi-so-mi-do-" may beckon listeners to its source, an old Baptist or Methodist church in the cove, where a "shaped-note sing" is being held. There, descendants of the mountain settlers, themselves now

old, join voices with the younger singers who have come to find their sense of place. And we listeners, standing in the cemetery on the hill beside the church, hear the music mark a mystic link with time. As they sing, our lives touch briefly with the people of the past. And with the music comes understanding: there really are no differences between us.

As every life style gives way eventually to change, so the isolated self-sufficiency of the mountain folk was not to last. As numbers of settlers grew, communities formed, each having a miller, blacksmith, and carpenter. Some coves in Tennessee had mail service by the mid-1800s, and

Tiny mountain churches were centers of spiritual and social life for small mountain communities. There are over 130 cemeteries in the park. Many are near church sites but some are private family cemeteries near old homesites. Homecoming is still celebrated in the Smokies. Gathering yearly to pay homage to their roots, families take part in the comforting traditions of singing, speech-making, dinner (on the ground), and lively conversations usually involving family kinships.

The logging era brought industrialism to the Smokies on a scale it had never known before. Railroads, built to haul away the fallen logs, defied ordinary limits of construction. This swinging railroad bridge was built to transport logs across the water at Meigs Creek and Little River.

by the time of the Civil War the Indian Gap road linked Sugarlands with Oconaluftee. The mountains were becoming tamer.

LUMBERING: A NEW ECONOMY

The prime agent in the taming—and denuding—of the mountains was the lumber industry. The huge, multi-specied forests of the Smokies represented a resource already scarce in an East whose forests had been stripped of their finer trees by large lumbering companies. In 1901 the Little River Lumber Company acquired 8,600 acres of land in the Little River section. During the next several years other lumber companies set up operations in the Eagle Creek, Hazel Creek, and Forney Creek areas of North Carolina. Then came the largest company, Champion Lumber, which acquired almost one-fifth of the present acreage of the park for its lumber operations.

The next twenty years saw the production of tremendous amounts of board-foot lumber from the forests of the Great Smokies. The forests were cut with little regard for the long-range effects of their destruction. Logs were "skidded" or dragged out by horses. They were "ball-hooted" or rolled downhill. There were "splash-dams," creeks

dammed so that the released flood would carry the logs downstream.

Railroads were built; towns sprang up; sawmills dotted the mountains. The present campgrounds of Elkmont and Smokemont, the areas of Tremont, and Greenbrier—these and other places that had been backwoods settlements were now bustling logging communities and mill towns, connected in several cases by railroads. (The present Little River road from Townsend to Elkmont campground is laid on top of the railroad bed.)

During all of this, the ways of the mountaineer had changed tremendously. Mountain people cut the trees, laid the roads, sawed the lumber. They sold their small tracts of land to the lumber companies and they sold goods or staples— honey, apples, butter, and eggs—to people in the towns and settlements. With their money they bought the goods for which they had bartered before, in a simpler time. Yet in many ways these gently proud mountain people clung tenaciously to their customs and traditions. They'd seen changes come and changes go, and some still preferred the "old ways."

There was no escaping the disruption wrought by the agents of industrialism. The lumber industry affected mountain dweller and forest wilderness. In both cases the alteration was a drastic one. Forests that had stood for centuries were leveled. Fires ravaged the mountainslopes. With little green protection, the downed slash was ready tinder. Without the understory growth to hold the rainfall, erosion washed the rich topsoil away, so that mountainsides slid after a heavy rainfall. Clingmans Dome, Silers Bald, Mount Guyot, all bear the scars of fires. Today a hiker at the Charlies Bunion or in the Sawteeth can look down the slope to see barren rock, all that was left after the fires and slides of the lumbering era.

Although two-thirds of the present park area was logged or burned, there were still pockets of virgin timber—enough to distinguish the area as the largest remaining virgin forest in the East. And the number of people who were determined that it would stay that way was growing.

The Making of a Park

The fact that the Great Smoky Mountains became a national park is due to the citizens of Tennessee and North Carolina who recognized the rich resource for what it was. It is also due to a few visionaries who proposed a national park and gave their time, efforts, and money to make sure it would become a reality.

Perhaps one of the first to recognize the Smokies was Horace Kephart, who wrote of his years in Deep Creek, Hazel Creek, and Bryson City in the book, *Our Southern Highlanders*. His prolific journalistic writings just after the turn of the century deplored the land's destruction by the lumber companies and advocated the establishment of a national park. These ideas helped to waken the public's consciousness, but it would take forty years for the proposal to become reality as a national park.

In 1923 a group formed in Knoxville to support the development of a national park in the Smokies. Mr. and Mrs. Willis P. Davis, Knoxville residents, had traveled to the country's western national parks, a trip that set Mrs. Davis to thinking about the magnificent wilderness in their own mountains and posing the question, "Why couldn't we have a park in the Smokies?" The Davises approached Colonel David Chapman, and together they formed the Great Smoky Mountains Conservation Association.

Acquiring land for a national park was not as easy to accomplish here as it had been in western areas. This land was almost entirely owned by small mountain farmers or big lumber companies still pulling enough lumber from the slopes to

NPS PHOTO

The great girth of the forest monarchs dwarfed the men who felled them. The yellow poplar was the most common and most profitable saw timber.

make them less than eager to sell the land. But two years later Congress, which had recently gone on record as opposing the purchase of lands for parks, yielded to public pressure and authorized the acquisition of land by organizations in Tennessee and North Carolina. The efforts began.

With the leadership of Colonel Chapman, the support in Washington of Arno Cammerer (then director of the National Park Service), and the eloquence of writers like Kephart, groups in North Carolina and Tennessee began to raise money to buy the land. There were school drives, community programs, and all manner of efforts by citizen groups in both states. By 1926, citizens had gathered over a million dollars. By 1927, the legislatures of each state had donated two million dollars.

Still the money raised was not enough; indeed a great deal more was needed. Much of this was forthcoming when Cammerer presented the park idea to his close friend, philanthropist John D. Rockefeller, who doubled the park fund by matching it with an additional five million dollars. And the year 1933 saw a federal allocation of over $1.5 million.

About 6,600 parcels of land within the proposed boundaries of the park were individually owned. Negotiations to obtain deeds for these separate properties was a huge task, complicated by personal feelings that often reached a high degree of emotional intensity. Some of the owners were mountain people who had lived here all their lives, as had their kin for generations before them, and they did not want to sell at any price. On the other hand, the land had not been generous, and to many people, especially those of the younger

*The John Oliver cabin in Cades Cove typifies
the craftsmanship, skill, and determination that built
a life in a world of "make do or do without."*

generation, the opportunity to sell was a good chance to move on to a better life.

The states had to resort to condemnation proceedings in order to buy the properties of those few who refused to sell. The harshness of these actions was tempered, however, by the fact that some of the older mountain people were assured that they could live out their lives in the homes they had always known.

And slowly the eighteen lumber companies were persuaded to sell their vast holdings. The last holdout was the largest land owner of all—Champion Lumber Company. When that company eventually sold its holdings, the three tallest peaks of the Smokies, with their still-virgin spruce forests, became part of what was destined to be an internationally famous botanical and recreational reserve.

June 15, 1934, was a red-letter day, when Con-

*The simplicity and gentle pride of the southern
highlander is eloquently revealed in the face of Aunt
Sophie Campbell, who for many years made and
sold clay pipes to the folks in the Gatlinburg area.*

NPS PHOTO

*The neat interior of the Walker sisters' cabin
in Little Greenbrier Cove exemplified the house-
keeping philosophy of "a place for everything
and everything in its place," a standard
essential to maintaining order in a two-room
cabin built to house a whole family.*

NPS PHOTO

Stretching toward the distant hills, a dirt road invites participation in the historic open-air "museum,"
Cades Cove. This mountain cove, like others in the Smokies, is a fertile valley surrounded by
mountains, with a single creek as its drainage. The mystique of Cades Cove lies in its remoteness; its
rich soil and gentle topography allowed a distinct mountain community to develop and thrive for 115 years.

Horses graze contentedly in a pastoral Cades Cove meadow.

gress authorized full development of the park. This is now the official birthday of the park, although it was not actually dedicated until September 2, 1940 (by President Franklin D. Roosevelt). The designation of the park had had to take a back burner temporarily, for although it had been recognized as the prime area for the East's first national park, accessibility and acquisition problems were such that Shenandoah National Park was the one to claim this distinction. Nevertheless, Great Smoky Mountains National Park was now a reality, and the efforts of thousands of people had been rewarded.

It had not been an easy accomplishment—but then, accomplishments of the greatest merit rarely are. Not only had a national recreation ground been provided, where millions could touch their natural and cultural roots, but a reserve of unequaled scientific value had been set aside. Moreover, the Smokies is a "museum" of a way of rural life that like the Cherokees' could not have long survived the onslaught of such a magnitude of new developments and change. For the wilderness and its inhabitants—and, perhaps, in the long run even for the mountaineers who left what they had loved—the change was a beneficial one.

The weathered barn was a symbol of growing prosperity for the pioneer-turned-farmer and a symbol of his role in the community. The wagon, usually much smaller than this one and sometimes just a flat sled with wooden runners, was an indispensable farm item. Hitched to a trusty mule, it could be used to haul wood, supplies, crops, critters, and people.

43

A variety of activities—from flower seeking to mountain climbing—make the Smokies a place that anyone can enjoy. Biking is a popular pastime along the eleven-mile loop drive around Cades Cove. In summer and fall, horses can be rented from riding stables in various parts of the park. Hiking trails and walkways offer gentle-to-strenuous gradients. And, of course, paved roads and dirt roads are always there for those who prefer a "windshield view" of this great mountain wilderness.

ED BOWER

TOMORROW'S HERITAGE

From a region once thought to be among the most isolated in the East, the Great Smoky Mountains has become the most visited national park in the country with approximately 10.2 million visits recorded in 1987. What brings so many here? Perhaps it is the rugged mountains, rich forests, and clear, free-flowing streams. Perhaps it is the appeal of a pioneer culture whose remnants are preserved within its coves. Perhaps it is the challenge of the wilderness, an urge to know the

Millions come to the Smokies to see the "fall color."

STEPHEN J. KRASEMANN

fullness of a land both beautiful and dangerous. Perhaps it is a deep-down longing for respite from a society whose technological advances are sometimes "too much with us." We may all come for different reasons, but most of us go home a little richer for the time that we have spent here.

In a park of 520,000 acres, nearly ninety percent is managed as wilderness. Visitors may hike the eight hundred miles of trails, fish the seven hundred miles of streams, camp in the numerous back-country sites and several developed campgrounds. They may view the park, and many do, from the wayside overlooks along the roads.

These and many other opportunities abound. But with the ever-increasing numbers of visitors come a host of problems that would make the early settlers of these hills scratch their heads in disbelief:

How do you break up a "bear jam" that has cars lined up for miles on either side? What do you do to lessen the congestion of hundreds of cars on a busy summer day? How do you deal with exotics, such as wild hogs or rainbow trout, that threaten the survival of rare plants and animals, disrupt natural systems, and compete with native species for a narrow niche in the ecosystem? In a back country that receives thousands of pairs of tramping feet each year, what measures do you take to protect the hikers *and* the land through which they walk? In short, what measures must be taken to ensure the continuation of the experiences for which over ten million visitors come?

The challenges of managing such an area are as diverse as the wilderness itself. Park managers

are considering optional forms of mass transportation to lessen traffic congestion. New methods are being tried to reduce confrontations between people and wildlife. Biologists and resource managers are continually studying populations of native species and experimenting with ways to control non-native ones, in order to maintain the tenuous balance in the forest communities.

Air and water quality are monitored, both on the ground and by satellite, to provide a set of data for measuring the impact of outside developments upon the environment of the park. In 1977 the park was designated an "International Biosphere Reserve" in recognition of the significance and integrity of its resources. As such a reserve, data concerning the condition of its air, water, soil, flora, and fauna is used as a baseline against which to monitor the intensity and effect of environmental changes occurring elsewhere as a result of global human impact. The park is within two days' drive of half of the population of the eastern United States; yet, even with the tremendous visitation the park now experiences, its resources remain essentially unimpaired.

There is something else—something more personal—that makes the Smokies a cherished place to visit. In an age of rapid transformation and increasing tempo, Great Smoky Mountains offers a haven, a retreat, a change from our everyday way of life. And to the especially perceptive it may offer some unique opportunities—to see wildlife in a truly wild environment, to discover that the wilderness experience is a way to know one-

Winter imbues the mountains with a magic quality and a visage totally different from its summer countenance. Although snowfall is infrequent at lower elevations, Newfound Gap and Clingmans Dome receive accumulations heavy enough for cross-country skiing and sledding—but best for simply watching the shimmering dance of icy trees illumined by shafts of sunlight piercing the frozen fog.

A hike of five and half miles— UP—ends at the rustic Mount LeConte Lodge (built before the park was established), where one may linger overnight, snug and dry among spruces, firs, and swirling mist on the third highest peak in the Smokies.

TO NEWPORT

FOOTHILLS PARKWAY

COSBY

32

40

321

32

TENNESSEE
NORTH CAROLINA

COSBY

BIG CREEK

GATLINBURG

GREENBRIER

40

TO ASHEVILLE

Mt. Le Conte
6593ft

CATALOOCHEE

Newfound Gap
5048ft

BALSAM
MOUNTAIN

276

CLINGMANS DOME
6642ft

SMOKEMONT

19

NATIONAL PARK

OCONALUFTEE

BLUE

VISITOR CENTER

441

RIDGE

CHEROKEE

19

TO WAYNESVILLE
AND ASHEVILLE

DEEP
CREEK

441

PARKWAY

BRYSON CITY

19

Ranger Station
Campground
Picnic Area
Pioneer Structure
Lookout Tower

Paved Road
Unpaved Road

TO WAYNESVILLE
AND ASHEVILLE

0   1   2   3   4   5

SCALE IN MILES

self as well as the land a little better, to share with others in a very special setting, to appreciate the tranquility of solitude in the silence of forests.

But perhaps the park's greatest importance is the option, the choice, it symbolizes to all of us simply by its existence. Just knowing that this park is here keeps alive within us the faith that opportunities to be close to nature do exist, and *will* exist—with careful stewardship—in the future. Great Smoky Mountains National Park thus preserves not only life and land, but offers the proof and promise of society's commitment to improving the quality of human life.

SUGGESTED READING

DUNN, DURWOOD. *Cades Cove.* Knoxville: University of Tennessee Press, 1988.

DYKEMAN, WILMA, AND STOKELY, JIM. *At Home in the Smokies.* Washington, D.C.: National Park Service, 1984.

KEPHART, HORACE. *Our Southern Highlanders.* Knoxville: University of Tennessee Press, 1922.

SHIELDS, RANDOLPH A. *The Cades Cove Story.* Gatlinburg: Great Smoky Mountains Natural History Ass'n., 1977.

AND LISTENING

CANTU, RITA. *I've Grown to Love This Land.* (Recorded Appalachian folk songs) Gatlinburg: Windance Productions, 1979.

The author gratefully acknowledges the assistance of Dr. Susan Bratton.

A crystalline fan of rime ice on slender trees unfolds across a wintry Smokies' sky.

ED BOWER

Books in this series: Acadia, Alcatraz Island, Arches, Blue Ridge Parkway, Bryce Canyon, Canyon de Chelly, Canyonlands, Cape Cod, Capitol Reef, Channel Islands, Civil War Parks, Crater Lake, Death Valley, Denali, Dinosaur, Everglades, Fort Clatsop, Gettysburg, Glacier, Glen Canyon-Lake Powell, Grand Canyon, Grand Canyon-North Rim, Grand Teton, Great Smoky Mountains, Haleakala, Hawaii Volcanoes, Lake Mead-Hoover Dam, Lassen Volcanic, Lincoln Parks, Mount Rainier, Mount Rushmore, Mount St. Helens, National Park Service, National Seashores, North Cascades, Olympic, Pecos, Petrified Forest, Redwood, Rocky Mountain, Scotty's Castle, Sequoia-Kings Canyon, Shenandoah, Statue of Liberty, Theodore Roosevelt, Virgin Islands, Yellowstone, Yosemite, Zion.

Published by KC Publications · Box 14883 · Las Vegas, NV 89114

Rain and mist lend an ethereal aura to a popular spot, Laurel Falls. Photo by David Muench

Back cover: The mountaineer way of life is demonstrated and preserved at the Pioneer Farmstead at Oconaluftee. Photo by Ed Cooper

Printed by Dong-A Printing Co., Ltd., Seoul, Korea
Separations by Color Masters